Searching
for
Hope

The Journey Study Series

Searching
for
Hope

A Thomas Nelson Study Series
Based on *The Journey*
by
BILLY GRAHAM

THOMAS NELSON
Since 1798

NASHVILLE   DALLAS   MEXICO CITY   RIO DE JANEIRO   BEIJING

Published in Nashville, Tennessee. Thomas Nelson is a trademark of Thomas Nelson, Inc.

Thomas Nelson, Inc., titles may be purchased in bulk for educational, business, fund-raising, or sales promotional use. For information, please e-mail SpecialMarkets@ThomasNelson.com.

Unless otherwise noted, all Scripture quotations are taken from *The Holy Bible*, NEW INTERNATIONAL VERSION®. NIV®. Copyright © 1973, 1978, 1984 by International Bible Society. Used by permission of Zondervan. All rights reserved.

Searching for Hope: A Thomas Nelson Study Series Based on The Journey *by Billy Graham*

ISBN-13: 978-1-4185-1659-8
ISBN-10: 1-4185-1659-7

Printed in the United States of America

07 08 09 10 11 RRD 5 4 3 2 1

Contents

1

The Universal Search

To get the most from this study guide, read the Preface and pages 3–12 of *The Journey*.

> *You and I are on a journey; we have been on it since the day we were born, and it won't end until our time on earth is finished. But what kind of journey will it be for you? The answer to that question is in your hands. You can't change the past, but with God's help you can change the future. He wants to free you from your old ways and put your feet on a new path—His path.*
>
> BILLY GRAHAM
> *The Journey*

THINK ABOUT IT

If you don't know where you're going, you will probably end up somewhere else.

—LAURENCE J. PETER[1]

*O LORD . . . if you will, please grant success to the journey
on which I have come.*

—GENESIS 24:42

Life is a journey . . . it has a beginning, a middle, and an end. The beginning is beyond our control. We can't choose when, where, or to whom we will be born. The end of life also is out of our control—at least the timing is. We do, however, have some control over what goes on in the meantime, between our birth and our death.

A universal search preoccupies the mind of almost every person, regardless of age, nationality, race, socioeconomic condition, or culture. It is a search for peace—for peace within our hearts and minds. It is a search also for peace between individuals, and between us and our Creator. This search is reflected in the ways people live and pursue their goals.

REWIND

What do you think is the number-one goal of most of the people you know?

_____ To obtain wealth

_____ To become successful

_____ To please God

_____ To have a good time

_____ To have loving relationships

_____ Other: _____

If someone determined your goals from your behavior, what might he or she assume is your primary goal in life?

_____ To obtain wealth

_____ To become successful

_____ To please God

_____ To have a good time

_____ To have loving relationships

_____ Other: _____

You are on a journey that began when you were conceived. Just as your journey had a beginning, it ultimately will have an end. Those are the two "givens" in this thing we call life. When this journey ends, we embark on another journey—one that will last forever! The choices you make on today's journey will determine your eternal journey.

If you were to die today, you would enter eternity. Based on your understanding right now, where will you spend eternity?

_____

_____

_____

Our immediate concerns can easily overshadow any thought of the future. We set our sights on becoming successful. But success, as the world defines it, often leaves people empty and searching. In the book *The Art of Possibility*, Benjamin and Rosamund Stone Zander define success as a "better place than where we are."[2] Sometimes that's the limit of our thinking—we aren't sure of anything other than the fact that we want life to be better.

On the scale that follows, place an X under the description that most accurately describes how you feel about your life.

Terrible   Not so good   Mediocre   Mostly good   Awesome

_____

Read Psalm 139:1–24 and consider God's plan for your life. In the space that follows, write a brief description of what you think God wants to do through your life.

_____

_____

_____

JOURNEY THROUGH GOD'S WORD

Psalm 139 was written by David and contains a mixture of wisdom and praise. It describes God's efforts to interact

---

with His creation. The psalm begins with a description of God's knowledge of the psalmist (vv. 1–6). In verses 7–12, David celebrates God's presence in his life. Verses 13–16—some of the most well-known in the book of Psalms—acknowledge God's involvement in the life process from the moment of conception. God's unlimited thoughts toward His creation are the subject of verses 17–18. In verses 19–22, David prays for punishment to fall upon those who are God's enemies. Finally, in verses 23–24, David prays that God would search his heart and lead him in God's ways.

The principles in this psalm are relevant to our daily lives:

1. God knows our innermost thoughts and loves us anyway.

2. God is with us in everything we do.

3. God knew us before we were born.

4. God thinks about us more than we think about Him.

5. The punishment of God's enemies is God's responsibility.

6. When we allow it, God will lead us in ways that are consistent with His character.

7. God wants to cleanse our lives of everything that keeps us from being what He wants us to be.

RETHINK

**Life is a journey—but what kind has it been so far for you?
Mark all the words that best describe your life journey.**

_____ happiness	_____ peace	_____ disappointment
_____ sorrow	_____ joy	_____ heartache
_____ excitement	_____ pleasure	_____ self-reliance
_____ boredom	_____ emptiness	_____ self-destruction
_____ unmet goals	_____ accomplishment	_____ sacrifice
_____ fame	_____ popularity	_____ unfulfilled

Lasting happiness and peace often are promised but seldom delivered. A bank once advertised its services with the slogan, "Happiness, security, peace of mind—we'll loan them to you!" That slogan accurately identified the things many people desire, but the promise was empty. The bank loaned money, but money can't deliver lasting happiness, security, or peace of mind.

Life can be overwhelming. Which of the following problems is a concern to you right now?

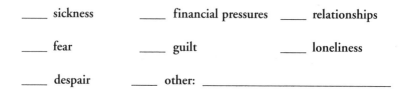

_____ sickness	_____ financial pressures	_____ relationships
_____ fear	_____ guilt	_____ loneliness
_____ despair	_____ other: _____	

Trouble is life's common denominator. The Old Testament figure Job knew that. In Job 5:7, he said, "Yet man is born to trouble as surely as sparks fly upward." But does life have to be troublesome? Some people seem to think so. They relish in anxiety and worry. If something isn't a big deal, they'll make it into one.

Deep inside, we all know that life doesn't have to be this way. Everyone wants life to be better, but few know the true source of real life.

What are some things people do to try to make their lives better?

_____

_____

_____

_____

It sounds simple, but different results require different actions. If you keep doing what you're doing, you'll keep getting what you're getting. Doing the same things will produce the same results. So, if you want life to be different, you must do something different. That's the idea behind repentance. Repentance simply means turning and going the opposite direction.

REFLECT

You aren't here by chance or by accident; you are here because God put you here. Long before the world was created, God knew all about you, and He planned to give you life. From all eternity you were part of His plan. No, you didn't have any choice about whether or not you would be born—but God had a choice about it, and He chose to give you life. Never forget: God put you on the journey.

BILLY GRAHAM
The Journey

If God only used perfect people, none of us would be usable. We all have failed, and we all come up short of God's standard. No matter where you are in life, you can begin again. Not only can you begin again, but you can make a difference in the world. There are three truths you must understand:

1. **God put you on this journey.**
   You are not a mistake, and you are not here by accident. If God didn't have a plan for you, why did He choose to leave you here? He chose when and where to place you; your life was His idea. In Jeremiah 1:5,

God told Jeremiah, "Before I formed you in the womb I knew you."

Read Jeremiah 29:11 and place "God" and "each person" in the appropriate blanks:

_____ has a plan for _____.

There are many people who have plans for God. Their prayer lives resemble placing an order at a drive-through window. They act as if they control God. Yet Jeremiah got it right when he acknowledged that God has a plan for each of us. Real joy is found when we pursue God's plan for our lives.

2. **God wants to join you on the journey.**
   In the beginning, it was God's desire to be in relationship with His creation. His desire hasn't changed. Because He loves you, He wants the best for you. And, He wants the best for you so much that He is willing to accompany you on your journey. Contrary to what many people believe, God is very interested in each of us. The fact that God is interested in us gives us hope for a better life.

Read the following Scriptures and summarize what each one says about God's closeness to us:

Deuteronomy 31:8

_____

_____

_____

_____

Matthew 28:20

_____

_____

_____

_____

Now that we know God's involvement in our lives, we must dig deeper to discover the specific tasks to which He has assigned each of us. Your assignment sometimes is referred to as your "calling."

Read 1 Corinthians 1:9. To what has God called you?

_____

_____

This comes as a surprise to some people. God called each of us into a relationship with His Son, Jesus Christ. We are part of His family! This leads us to the third truth.

3. **God calls you to a new journey.**

    Whatever you have experienced apart from a relationship with God is nothing compared to the joy and peace He has planned for you. The new journey won't be void of challenges and difficulties, but it will be void of the aimlessness that is so evident today.

Consider your present path. Where will you be . . .

. . . in one year?

_____

_____

. . . in five years?

_____

_____

. . . in twenty years?

_____

_____

. . . in eternity?

_____

_____

With all of the changes occurring in our world, it's difficult to project where we'll be tomorrow. Today's certainties often become tomorrow's uncertainties.

How certain are you about each of the following?
(1=not sure at all, 5=100% positive.)

World peace	1	2	3	4	5
Job security	1	2	3	4	5
Your next vacation	1	2	3	4	5
The weather	1	2	3	4	5
Your eternal destination	1	2	3	4	5

Can you be sure about any of the items on the list above? If so, which one(s)?

_____

_____

There is one thing on the list about which you can be sure—your eternal destination. You will spend eternity somewhere, and you get to decide where that will be.

REACT

Some people might argue that all religions ultimately lead to the same God. We live in a culture that embraces "spirituality" while rejecting the God of the Bible. Why should you agree to take the journey with God instead of traveling it by yourself? Let's look at some reasons:

1. **The old path will never deliver what it promises.**
   The old path leads to a self-centered life that might look satisfying on the outside, but on the inside is full of anxiety, fear, heartache, boredom, and sorrow. People become enslaved to their possessions and lifestyles. This isn't a new problem.

Read Luke 12:19-20. What was wrong with the path the man chose?

_____

_____

_____

2. **God's path always delivers what He promises.**
   The Bible doesn't promise you will be successful as the world defines success. It does, however, promise peace in the midst of chaos, purpose in the midst of uncertainty, and an abundant life!

Read Philippians 4:7 and describe the peace that God promises.

_____

_____

_____

Whenever I am traveling, I constantly look forward to the moment when I will return home. Even if I'm very busy and preoccupied, in the back of my mind one thought is always present: "Soon I'll be going home!" Home is a place of peace and security and rest; home is where I belong. How much greater should be our longing for our eternal home! Our true home is heaven—and that is where God's path leads.

BILLY GRAHAM
The Journey

3. **God's path will lead you home.**

As complex as life is, there really are only two paths— the path to heaven and the path to hell. There are few people who willingly choose hell as their eternal destination; yet, there are many people who desire heaven but refuse to get on the road that leads there.

Read Hebrews 11:13–16. God has prepared a place for you—heaven—and He invites you to come along on the journey to that destination. What has been your response to God's invitation?

_____ Yes   ___ No

Jesus said, "I have come that they may have life, and have it to the full" (John 10:10). You can begin life's journey afresh by committing your life to Christ and learning to walk with Him every day. This is the one thing about which you can be certain. By accepting God's offer of salvation through a personal relationship with Jesus Christ, you can know where you will spend eternity. You also can experience His presence and guidance every day as you learn to walk with Him. If you have never done so, ask Him to come into your life today.

What are three truths you learned in this study lesson, and how will you apply each truth to your daily life?

1. _____

_____

_____

_____

2. _____

   _____

   _____

   _____

3. _____

   _____

   _____

   _____

2

The
Search
for God

To get the most from this study guide, read the Preface and pages 13–18 of *The Journey*.

> *God isn't trying to hide from us. Quite the opposite: God wants us to know He exists. Not only that, He wants us to know what He is like.*
>
> BILLY GRAHAM
> *The Journey*

THINK ABOUT IT

The longer I live, the more convincing proofs I see of the truth—that God governs the affairs of men. . . . We have been assured, sir, in the sacred writings, that "except the Lord build the house, they labour in vain that build it."

—BENJAMIN FRANKLIN[1]

O LORD, our Lord,
    how majestic is your name in all the earth!
You have set your glory
    above the heavens.

—PSALM 8:1

Where is God? Who is God? Those questions occupy the minds of people who want tangible proof of God's existence. Yet, because God made us, we can never really understand ourselves without a basic understanding of God.

But people have different ideas about God—some logical, some very fanciful or even contradictory. For many, God is something like a genie in a bottle. For others, He is an angry authoritarian judge waiting to punish His subjects. You probably have some ideas about God. But are your ideas accurate?

REWIND

Based on the way you live, which analogy best describes your concept of God?

_____ Angry law-enforcement officer

_____ Strict judge

_____ Generous grandfather

_____ Company CEO

_____ Distant relative

____ Loving father

____ Other: _____

Based on your understanding of Scripture, which analogy best describes God?

____ Angry law-enforcement officer

____ Strict judge

____ Generous grandfather

____ Company CEO

____ Distant relative

____ Loving father

____ Other: _____

Is there a difference between the two concepts of God? If so, why?

_____

_____

_____

Some people believe that God wants to be hidden and distant from us. But that's not true. God *wants* us to know what He is like. We don't have to wonder or guess; God already has revealed Himself to us. We can discover a lot about God by looking at the clues He provides.

> *Unfortunately, most speculations about God miss one very important truth: God wants us to know what He is like. We don't need to guess, because God has revealed Himself to us. We know He exists because He has left clues behind for us to discover.*
>
> BILLY GRAHAM
> *The Journey*

Match the following Scripture passages with their statements: [Answers can be found at the end of the chapter.]

a. God has given us rain and crops.

b. Creation gives evidence of God's existence.

c. The moon and the stars are evidence of God's existence.

_____ Romans 1:20   _____ Psalms 8:3

_____ Acts 14:17

Some people might argue that God doesn't exist because He can't be proven to exist physically. Yet, there are many things in life that we can't prove yet we believe to be true. You believe George

Washington was real, yet you have never seen him. You believe man walked on the moon, but you weren't there. We believe these historical facts because of the testimonies of witnesses and the residual evidence.

Today you can know God exists because of the testimonies of witnesses and the residual evidence. The witnesses to God's existence date back to the dawn of creation and include modern-day people who have seen God at work in their lives. The residual evidence exists in the sunrise and sunset of each day, the changing of the seasons, and the mysteries that have no explanation other than God's hand.

In the space that follows, list some things people believe to be true but cannot prove.

JOURNEY THROUGH GOD'S WORD

Psalm 115 is a psalm of praise that focuses on the comparison between faith in the idols of the pagan culture and faith in the God of Creation. Many of the passages found in Psalm 115 are duplicated in Psalm 135. Psalm 115 has the characteristics of a responsive reading that would have been used in corporate worship.

Psalm 115 contains five movements:

1. Praise to God (vv. 1–2)

2. Comparison between the false gods and God (vv. 3–8)

3. An expression of trust in God (vv. 9–11)

4. An expression of God's blessing (vv. 12–15)

5. God's present and future glorification (vv. 16–18)

This psalm combats many thoughts that were present then and still exist today. The first movement counters the tendency for people to take glory for themselves that rightfully belongs to God. The second movement counters the tendency to create our own gods. The third movement calls for people to remember to trust God, not themselves. The fourth movement reminds us that God is the source of all blessings. Finally, the fifth movement calls worshipers to remember that God is the focus of all creation past, present, and future.

As you can see, the Psalms (and all of the Bible) spoke God's truth to the original audience and continue to speak God's truth to us today!

RETHINK

No matter where we look, we see God's footprints. Think about your daily routine. List some places and/or situations in which you might see God's footprints.

_____

_____

_____

_____

But seeing God's footprints isn't enough; we need to hear from Him. Just seeing evidence of someone's existence doesn't reveal that person's character. To really get to know someone, you must have a conversation and a relationship with that person. That's exactly what God desires, so He has spoken to us and made a way for us to have a relationship with Him.

What are some things people do to try to have a relationship with God?

____ Go to church   ____ Read religious books

____ Watch religious television   ____ Pray

_____ Wear religious jewelry   _____ Use religious words

_____ Use meditation techniques   _____ Listen to religious music

_____ Consult astrology charts

_____ Other: _____

How often do you communicate with God?

Sometimes

Never -- All the time

Not all of the actions above are bad (although some are); yet they aren't the causes of a real relationship with God. You don't go to church to obtain a relationship with God; you go to church *because of* your relationship with God. A real relationship with God is the result of our engaging Him in communication.

When do you most often talk to God?

_____ Before a meal   _____ When I'm in trouble

_____ At church   _____ On holidays

_____ When I'm forced to   _____ Daily during my quiet time

_____ All the time

If you communicated with other people as often as you communicate with God, what kind of relationships would you have? When we look at it like that, we can see why we don't have closer relationships with God. It's not because God isn't talking; it's because we aren't investing time in the relationship.

REFLECT

> *You might learn something about me if you saw me walking down the street (you would at least conclude I exist!). You would learn even more by watching me work. But you would only discover what I was really like if we sat down and talked. The same is true with God. We need Him to speak to us— and He has! God has spoken to us in words we can understand, and those words are found in the Bible.*
>
> BILLY GRAHAM
> *The Journey*

God isn't hiding from us. As we have seen, He reveals Himself to us through the world He created. However, He also reveals Himself to us in the words He speaks to us. Because God never changes, the words that are recorded in the Bible still apply to every person on the earth. Let's look at the ways God has spoken to us.

1. **God has spoken to us through a book: the Bible.**
   The Bible is a collection of books written over hundreds of years by many different authors. The authors, however, were inspired by the Spirit of God to communicate His message. Therefore, the message reveals God's character and His love for all humanity.

Read Hebrews 1:1. Through what people and in how many ways did God speak?

_____

_____

_____

Read 2 Peter 1:20–21. What inspired the prophets to speak?

_____

_____

_____

God wants to communicate with us so much that He left us His Word in language we can understand.

2. **God has spoken to us through a Person: Jesus Christ.**

    Jesus Christ, God's Son, came to this earth for one purpose—to reconcile humanity to God. In doing so, Jesus spoke directly to people. Many of His words are recorded in the first four books of the New Testament. Like the Old Testament writers, Jesus spoke to a specific culture, but His words contain truths that are relevant to every culture in every age.

More than that, Jesus Christ was God Incarnate—God in human flesh. Do you want to know what God is like? Look at Jesus Christ, because "God was pleased to have all his fullness dwell in him" (Colossians 1:19).

Read the following Scriptures and summarize what each one says about Jesus' identity:

Colossians 2:9

_____

_____

_____

John 1:14

_____

_____

_____

We can see that God wants us to know who He is. He isn't trying to play games with us! We can know God in a personal way. We can spend time with Him. We can have conversations with Him. We can know God by knowing His Son, Jesus Christ.

REACT

There is a difference between knowing about someone and knowing that person. Many people suggest that ours is a Christian culture, yet the evidence doesn't support the claim. Certainly there are many people in our culture who know about God, yet there are far fewer who actually know God. Maybe it would be a good idea to remind yourself of your history with God.

1. **Describe your life before you had a relationship with God.**

   _____

   _____

   _____

   _____

2. What was it that made you realize your need for God?

_____

_____

_____

_____

_____

3. Describe when and how you asked for forgiveness and invited Jesus Christ into your life.

_____

_____

_____

_____

_____

4. How has your life been different since that time? What difference does God make in your daily life?

_____

_____

_____

_____

_____

If you struggled with your responses to the questions above, you might need to reevaluate your relationship with God. Many people go through life thinking they have settled the issue, but they have never made a conscious choice to ask Jesus Christ into their lives. Knowing God means being intimately acquainted with His Word and His ways. Knowing God means giving Him total control of your life. Knowing God means waking every morning with the assurance that you will spend eternity with Him in heaven. Do you have that assurance?

Through His Word and His Son, God has spoken about your past, your present, and your future. Because He loves you, He pursues you. Yet many people refuse to accept God's love.

Why might people choose to reject God's love?

_____ They don't consider themselves worthy of His love.

_____ They don't believe God exists.

_____ They assume they will have time for God when they grow old.

_____ They have never heard about God.

_____ They like life the way it is.

_____ They don't see evidence of God's making a difference in the lives of people who claim to know Him.

_____ Other: _____

Have any of the thoughts above ever been your thoughts?

_____ Yes   _____ No

What happened to change your thinking?

_____

_____

_____

The fact that God has spoken to us reveals a lot about God's attitude toward us. God didn't have to reveal anything to us. We aren't entitled to know Him. He communicates with us because of who He is, not who we are.

Read Psalm 8:1–5. In this passage, the psalmist speaks about several ways God demonstrates His love for His people. Rewrite this passage expressing your thoughts about the ways in which God demonstrates His love to you.

_____

_____

_____

_____

Because God loves us, He has some things He wants to tell us. His desires for us are expressed in the words He spoke through the Bible and through His Son. No matter where we look, we see evidence of God's desire to communicate with us. Knowing that God has spoken to us is important, but what did He say and why did He say it? We'll learn more about the specifics of God's message in future lessons.

> *We can know what God is like, because He wants us to know Him.*
>
> BILLY GRAHAM
> *The Journey*

What are three truths you learned in this study, and how will you apply each truth to your daily life?

1. _____

_____

_____

_____

2. _____

_____

_____

_____

3. _____

_____

_____

_____

Answers to Scripture matching on page 26 —

a. Acts 14:17; b. Psalm 8:3; c. Romans 1:20

3

What
Is
God Like?

T O GET THE MOST FROM THIS STUDY GUIDE, READ pages 18–22 of *The Journey*.

We can't fully understand God. He is far greater than we are. He is infinite and we are finite. Only in heaven will we see Him in all of His fullness.

BILLY GRAHAM
The Journey

THINK ABOUT IT

What peace it brings to the Christian's heart to realize that our heavenly Father never differs from Himself. In coming to Him at any time, we need not wonder whether we shall find Him in a receptive mood. He is always receptive to misery and need, as well as to love and faith. He does not keep office hours nor set aside periods when He will see no one.

—A. W. TOZER[1]

I am God, and not man—the Holy One among you.

—HOSEA 11:9

As much as we might try, we cannot define God. In defining Him, we place boundaries around Him or limit Him. But we know God cannot be limited. So, how can we know what God is like? God has revealed His nature to us. Therefore, understanding more about God requires us to consider His characteristics as revealed in Scripture.

We make a mistake when we describe God in human terms. Humans are limited physically, mentally, and emotionally; yet God has no limits. Only when we understand His greatness will we understand our smallness.

So there is a distance between God and humanity. That might lead you to believe that it is impossible to know what God is like. Well, that's partly true! We can never fully know what God is like, but we can know more about Him by learning four important truths that He wants us to understand.

REWIND

From what sources have you developed your concepts about God?

_____ Television and/or movies

_____ Music

_____ Books

_____ Conversations with people

_____ The Bible

_____ Nature

_____ Personal experiences

_____ Other: _____

Complete the following statement: To me, God is like . . .

_____

_____

_____ .

How do you think your responses compare to God's true character? Do you think you might have any misconceptions about God? Where did those ideas originate, and are you open to changing your ideas about God?

Throughout history, godly men and women have written thousands of pages in an attempt to explain God. The insights shared in these volumes range from basic to bizarre. Honestly, it is very easy to get confused by all of the varying viewpoints. Therefore, we must rely on God's revelation in His Word for our information. We can be certain that God never changes; the character of God that is revealed in Scripture is still His character today.

Read the following Scriptures. What does each say about God?

Psalm 102:27

_____

_____

_____

Malachi 3:6

_____

_____

_____

Hebrews 1:12

_____

_____

_____

James 1:17

_____

_____

_____

The message is consistent—God never changes! God reminded us of this fact throughout Scripture. For the people who lived during the Old Testament and New Testament eras, this message of divine consistency was new. The pagan religions of the day worshiped gods that were humanlike. They were moody, inconsistent, distant, and often unapproachable. The gods fought and died. New gods were identified to replace old gods or to cover other areas of life. The spiritual culture lacked stability.

Today's culture isn't much different. There is a lot of confusion about God's identity and character. Let's take a look at four undeniable truths about God.

Truth One: God Is a Spirit

This is one of the most difficult truths for us to understand. Because God is a spirit, He can't be confined to a place or a time. He can't be seen or touched. Yet, He is real! Though we can't see God, we can see evidence of His existence and His work through His Spirit.

Because He is a spirit, God isn't limited by time or space. If you have been trying to limit God, don't! Don't try to confine Him to one place, or paint an imaginary picture of Him in your mind, or restrict Him to one way of doing things. Don't put limits on His power or greatness or love or wisdom. Limiting God is like looking at a mud puddle and thinking it's the ocean.

BILLY GRAHAM
The Journey

What do you think of when you hear the word *spirit*?

_____ Halloween

_____ Ghosts

_____ Make-believe

_____ A horror movie

_____ Psychics and fortune-tellers

_____ God

_____ Other: _____

How does your concept of "spirit" affect your ideas about God?

_____

_____

_____

In a world that was heavily influenced by pagan religion, the concept of a spiritual God was hard to grasp. Even when Jesus explained the idea, people still didn't understand. The same is true today. To the Samaritan woman, Jesus said, "God is spirit" (John 4:24). Following His death, burial, and resurrection, Jesus said to His disciples, "A ghost does not have flesh and bones" (Luke 24:39). These statements are still valid today.

JOURNEY THROUGH GOD'S WORD

God's leadership of His people always has been accomplished spiritually. When the Israelites left Egypt headed for the Promised Land, God led them by day and by night. In Exodus 13:17–22, we see the manifestation of God in a cloud and in fire. In this passage, we learn a few things about God and His plan for His people.

1. **God's path isn't always the most logical path.**

   The quickest path from Egypt to Canaan was due east. That path, however, would have taken the Israelites through Philistia—the land of the dreaded Philistines. In Exodus 13:17, God revealed His reasoning. God knew that a war with the Philistines would drive the Israelites back to Egypt. Does it ever seem as if God is taking you on the long path to a destination? If so, be encouraged by knowing that His plans are for your best interest.

2. **God's direction is definite.**

   Sometimes we act as if discovering God's direction for our lives is something like a game show in which we have to find the right door or we lose. The only thing that makes discovering God's path difficult is our reluctance to obey His instructions. The Israelites were led by God in a supernatural way—the cloud by day and the fire by night (Exodus 13:21–22). God still is in the supernatural leadership business. He isn't confused about His plans for you. He simply wants you to trust His leadership.

3. **God's leadership is constant.**

   God did not remove the cloud or the fire from before the Israelites. Not seeing the cloud and the fire would be the result of their turning away from God, not God's turning away from them (Exodus 13:22). Because God is consistent, His ways are the same today. Maybe He doesn't use clouds and pillars, but He still has a plan for your life. His plan is before you. If you don't see it, you might be facing the wrong direction. Don't make the mistake of looking for God's direction in horoscopes or cards. Don't let your mind limit what God can do through you.

Every trait we attribute to ourselves can be attributed to God. A person feels, thinks, desires, and decides—and so does God. A person enters into relationships—and so does God. A person acts—and so does God. God feels; God thinks; God sympathizes; God forgives; God hopes; God decides; God acts; God judges—all because He is a person. God is not an impersonal force or power; He is a person—the most perfect person imaginable.

BILLY GRAHAM
The Journey

Truth Two: God Is a Person

God has a personality with the same characteristics as ours. Just like a person, God thinks, feels, desires, and decides. He enters into relationships and loves. He is sympathetic and judicious. The only difference is that God is perfect in all His ways. So, when God thinks, He thinks perfectly. When He decides, it is always the right decision. The Bible teaches that God's "works are perfect, and all his ways are just" (Deuteronomy 32:4).

Which of your personality traits are most like God's?

____ Feeling	____ Acting	____ Judging
____ Thinking	____ Sympathizing	____ Loving
____ Deciding	____ Forgiving	____ Accepting
____ Desiring	____ Hoping	____ Giving

Circle the personality traits that need transforming by God. What can you do to allow God to transform these traits?

_____

_____

_____

Truth Three: God Is Holy

Holy means set apart for a purpose. The standard for holiness is God; anything else simply doesn't measure up. Though we might try, we can never be as holy as God. Whereas we can participate in evil, God cannot look upon it. That's the difference between His holiness and ours. Our holiness is volatile; God's is steady.

When we look at life from our perspectives, we don't see sin for what it is. Culturally, we rationalize certain behaviors and attitudes so that they are no longer considered sin. From God's perspective, however, things haven't changed. His holiness prevents Him from excusing sin.

What are some things our culture accepts that God still condemns?

_____

_____

_____

_____

_____

What have been some of the consequences of this change in social attitude?

_____

_____

_____

Read the following Scripture verses. Summarize each verse in the space provided.

Habakkuk 1:13

_____

_____

_____

Isaiah 6:3

_____

_____

_____

1 John 1:5

_____

_____

_____

Revelation 4:8

_____

_____

_____

Based on the verses you read, what can you conclude about God's character?

_____

_____

_____

_____

Truth Four: God Is Love

We know that God cannot look upon sin and that He is just in all His ways. So, why do we have hope for today and tomorrow? Because of God's love. God doesn't possess love; He *is* love. The Bible says that "God is love" (1 John 4:8). Since love is a characteristic of God, we know that it is perfect.

It is difficult to see love, but we can see the effects of it. It was love that gave humanity a second chance following the sin of Adam and Eve in the Garden of Eden. Love prompted God to save Noah and his family from the Flood. Love sustained the Israelites through their forty years of wandering in the desert. Love delivered a Savior wrapped in flesh. Love allowed God's Son to be crucified in spite of His innocence. Love resurrected Him to give us hope. Love overwhelms our hearts when we come face to face with the God of the universe.

Go back and substitute "God" for "love" in the paragraph above and you'll see that the truth is unchanged because God is love. John put it this way: "This is love: not that we loved God, but that he loved us and sent his Son as an atoning sacrifice for our sins" (1 John 4:10).

What are some things love does in your life?

_____

_____

Is it easy to see God doing those same things? Why or why not?

_____

_____

_____

RETHINK

Descriptions define the boundaries of an item or a concept. Therefore, any attempt to define God violates the very concept of God because He has no limits or boundaries. Every descriptive term used of God is inadequate because our terminology is limited to things we understand.

God's love isn't the same as our love. In the context of His love, God exercises judgment and punishes sin. Eventually, we all come to understand that everything God does is rooted in His love for us and His desire to be in a relationship with us.

Read Jeremiah 31:3. Which of these terms best describe your reaction to this verse?

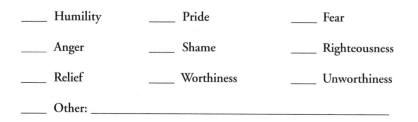

____ Humility   ____ Pride   ____ Fear

____ Anger   ____ Shame   ____ Righteousness

____ Relief   ____ Worthiness   ____ Unworthiness

____ Other: _____

In what do you place your hope? Your employer? Your degrees? Your friends? Your family? Your church? Your physical appearance? Your retirement account? As secure as you might feel, nothing compares to the eternal security that comes from knowing Jesus Christ as your Savior and Lord.

As you reflect on your relationship with God, can you see evidence of His activity in your life? Today are you more like Him than you were when your relationship with Him began?

What has happened that has caused you to grow closer to God?

_____

_____

_____

What has happened that has caused you to move away from God?

_____

_____

_____

REFLECT

Hope is defined as "a wish or desire accompanied by confident expectation of its fulfillment." Your wishes and desires are rooted in some aspect of your life. We all need hope for today, for tomorrow, and for eternity.

Why do people place their hope in things other than God?

_____

_____

_____

What has kept you from living with hope in God?

_____

_____

_____

REACT

When you begin to better understand who God is, you will respond in one of the following ways:

1. **Walk away because your hope is in something else.**
   Jesus offered a kind of hope that never had been offered before. Much like it is in our culture, hope often was associated with financial or social status.

   Read Matthew 19:16–22. In what was the young man's hope?

   _____

   _____

   _____

   How would you have responded in a similar situation?

   _____

   _____

   _____

   _____

2. **Place your hope in Jesus Christ and live in obedience to Him.**
   This is the only other choice. Choosing to wait until later is the same as walking away from God.

Read Acts 8:26–40. How did the decision of the Ethiopian differ from that of the rich young man in Matthew 19?

_____

_____

_____

Spiritually, are you more like the rich young man or the Ethiopian? Explain your response.

_____

_____

_____

If it weren't for God's love, we would have no hope, either in this life or in the life to come. But there is hope because He loves us.

BILLY GRAHAM
The Journey

What are three truths you learned in this study, and how will you apply each truth to your daily life?

1. _____

_____

_____

_____

2. _____

_____

_____

_____

3. _____

_____

_____

_____

4

Who Am I?

To GET THE MOST FROM THIS STUDY GUIDE, READ pages 23–27 of *The Journey.*

We are incomplete without God. If we leave Him out of our lives, we have an empty place in our souls, a yearning deep inside us that only God can satisfy. No matter how hard we try, if we ignore God that hollow place stays with us, and our search for lasting peace and happiness will be futile.

BILLY GRAHAM
The Journey

THINK ABOUT IT

God tells man who he is. God tells us that He created man in His image. So man is something wonderful.

—FRANCIS SCHAEFFER[1]

Abraham . . . was called God's friend.

—JAMES 2:23

You were created to know God and to be His friend forever. God didn't set the world in motion and then abandon it. He had something in mind before the first light broke through the darkness.

It might not seem like it, but everything exists for a purpose—including you! There are plenty of examples of things being used for purposes other than those designed by God. That's a result of sin in our world. The very fact that you exist says that God has a plan that involves you. Otherwise, you wouldn't be here.

We all have an inner desire for friendship. But with whom or what are you trying to be friends? The answer to that question will provide some spiritual clues about your life. If you are pursuing anything more than you are pursuing God, you will never find real peace. Only after you make your friendship with God your first priority will your calling and direction in life become clearer. You don't have to go through life in a personal fog; you can live the way God intended you to live.

It is the greatest discovery you will ever make. You were created to know God and to be His friend forever. You and I weren't put here just to be preoccupied with ourselves—our own problems and pleasure. We weren't even put here just to make this a better world (although that has its place). The Great Designer had a Great Design: that we might know Him and be His friends forever.

BILLY GRAHAM
The Journey

REWIND

Which statement best characterizes your relationship with God?

_____ We are strangers.

_____ We are casual acquaintances.

_____ We have a professional relationship.

_____ He is my life-mechanic; I call on Him when something is broken.

_____ We are friends.

_____ Other: _____

If your friends and/or family members were asked the same question about you, what would they say?

_____ Their perception of me would be the same as mine.

_____ They would see my relationship with God differently than I see it.

Everyone is searching for meaning in life. Just browse the self-help section at your local bookstore and you'll find a growing inventory of books that offer help with your search. Maybe you, like the writer of Ecclesiastes, have concluded that life can be "meaningless, a chasing after the wind" (Ecclesiastes 1:14).

Life, however, doesn't have to be this way. The solution begins with a better understanding about who you are in light of God's grand scheme.

Describe yourself by completing this statement: I am . . .

_____

Now go back and circle the word _God_ in your description. Did you include God when describing yourself? Why or why not?

_____

_____

_____

_____

You are incomplete apart from God because your identity is rooted in Him. He knew you before you were born and ordained your days. Your life isn't yours to control; God has a project for which you are the perfect tool. Trying to live apart from God, therefore, is frustrating because you never realize your real purpose in life. There is a void within each person that only God can fill.

What makes your heart restless?

_____

_____

_____

_____

Read Augustine's quote on page 24 in *The Journey*. What was his answer to that question?

_____

_____

_____

_____

This inner restlessness is the result of man's separation from God. The separation became a part of our existence when Adam and Eve were disobedient to God in the Garden of Eden. It's a problem that everyone attempts to solve but not always in the same way.

JOURNEY THROUGH GOD'S WORD

We encounter the concept of knowledge throughout God's Word. Though we might consider knowledge academic in nature, the biblical writers had something else in mind. In addition to the intellectual aspects, knowledge included experience, emotion, and various kinds of relationships.

When the Bible refers to God's knowledge, it includes both the range of God's knowledge and the depth of His knowledge. Genesis tells us that God knows our pasts. In Job 31:4, we learn that God knows our present situations. In Luke 1:33, we see that God knows the future. When it comes to the depth of God's knowledge, Psalm 147:5 teaches that God's understanding is superior to anyone's understanding.

Knowing God is more than acknowledging His existence or even His power. Knowing God is the primary responsibility of humanity. It is more than an academic knowledge; it is experiential. It is not theoretical; it is based on the facts that grow out of one's personal experiences with God. Knowledge of God always leads to the worship of God.[2]

The perfect relationship between God and humanity existed when Adam and Eve were in the Garden of Eden before they sinned. Adam and Eve also had perfect relationships with each other. God met their every need, and they had nothing to interfere with their commitment to Him.

What interferes with your relationship with God?

_____

_____

_____

RETHINK

What does it mean to be created in God's image?

_____ It means I'm in control of my life.

_____ It means I decide what's right and wrong.

_____ It means I am designed to be in relationship with my Creator.

_____ It means God left me here to figure things out on my own.

_____ **Other:** _____

Being created in God's image means having a spiritual and a physical nature. Take a look at Genesis 1:27. God had no physical nature, so our being created in the image of God says more about our spiritual nature than our physical nature. It stands to reason that God's inclusion of the spiritual nature means that His concern for us always has a spiritual purpose.

If we think we are only sophisticated animals, we will begin to act like sophisticated animals. But if we realize we were created in God's image and have a God-given soul, we won't live like animals. Our souls make us uniquely human, and they give dignity and value to every human life. Most of all, our souls are the part of us that can experience God and have fellowship with Him. We were equipped by our Creator not only to live on this earth, but also to live in touch with heaven.

BILLY GRAHAM
The Journey

God deliberately created Adam and Eve to be His friends forever. God didn't have to create Adam and Eve, but He did. Because He created us, God desires to be in a right relationship with His creation. What makes us different from other aspects of creation is the spiritual capacity. Humans have a soul. How important is your soul? Our souls are eternal. In other words, the spiritual portion of you will never die.

Read Matthew 16:26. What two priorities did Jesus mention?

1. _____

2. _____

For you, which of the priorities listed above is more important? Why?

_____

_____

_____

_____

What is the one thing you do most during an average day?

_____

_____

_____

_____

What is your primary motivation for doing that thing?

_____

_____

_____

When you read Psalm 8:5, you get a glimpse of the value God places on every human life. That verse says, "You made him a little lower than the heavenly beings and crowned him with glory and honor."

In light of this verse, what should be your attitude toward other people?

_____

_____

_____

You can live with dignity and hope because your Creator values you. Because you have the capacity to be in a relationship with God, you don't have to live in isolation or confusion. Rather, you have the opportunity to live as God's friend. That was God's design from the very beginning.

The presence of a soul makes humanity different from other life, but why did God create you? There is only one answer to that question—love! Not only did God create Adam and Eve, but He created the perfect place for them to live. But why? Love . . . that's it!

It's easier to say the word *love* than it is to understand it. We tend to view love from a limited human viewpoint. We love chocolate, dogs, football, and other people. We say we love a lot of things, and we even believe we are loved. Yet we don't understand how God's love compares to ours. Our love is imperfect; God's love is perfect.

Read Psalm 18:30. How do God's ways of doing things compare to our ways?

_____ Our ways are superior to God's.

_____ They are the same.

_____ God's ways are superior to ours.

What does this mean in regard to the way God loves us?

_____

_____

_____

Remember, human love is imperfect; God's love is perfect. Therefore, there are some things that we can't understand about God's love. But we don't have to understand everything in order to understand some things about God's love. We know that God didn't need to create us because He was lonely. His love compelled Him to fashion everything that was created. The creation of humanity was God's way of giving an outlet to His love. But why us?

What criteria do you use when selecting a friend?

_____ Appearance

_____ Age

_____ Interests

_____ Socioeconomic status

_____ Common dreams and goals

_____ Children are friends

_____ Same work

_____ Same church

_____ Social acquaintances

_____ Other: _____

Why does God want to be friends with you?

_____

_____

_____

_____

God created us to be His friends. Usually, friendship exists on a parallel plane. In other words, we tend to develop friendships with people who are somewhat like us. Yet in the friendship between God and humanity, the relationship isn't parallel. God is the Creator; we are the creation. God is limitless; we are limited. God is independent; we are dependent. Yet God still wants to be friends with us.

How does it make you feel to know that God wants to be your friend?

_____

_____

_____

_____

What are some things you should do to maintain your friendship with God?

_____

_____

_____

Why is it so difficult to do these things?

_____

_____

_____

REFLECT

Why do so many people miss this truth? Is it too simple, too spiritual, too unbelievable? Think about all of the things in life that promise happiness and fulfillment. Yet in most cases, happiness involves purchasing a product, service, or book. Politicians even promise peace in exchange for your vote. But these all are empty promises.

What things have you found yourself drawn to in your search for fulfillment?

_____ Sex   _____ Drugs   _____ Alcohol

_____ Fame   _____ Money   _____ Possessions

_____ Power   _____ Success

_____ Other: _____

What happened to make you realize that your search was in vain?

_____

_____

_____

_____

Your search will never end until you accept the fact that you were created to be God's friend. God doesn't want you to know *about* Him; He wants you to *know* Him. There is a big difference!

REACT

Read Proverbs 18:24. How does being God's friend affect your daily life? (Place an X on the line.)

Not at all |----------|----------|-----------|----------| It affects everything.

Read John 15:15. What is Jesus' attitude toward those who trust in Him as Savior and Lord?

_____

_____

_____

_____

_____

> *God is complete in Himself; He lacks nothing. But His love compelled Him to create the human race.*
>
> BILLY GRAHAM
> *The Journey*

What are three truths you learned in this study, and how will you apply each truth to your daily life?

1. _____

_____

_____

_____

2. _____

_____

_____

_____

3. _____

_____

_____

_____

5

Starting Over

T O GET THE MOST FROM THIS STUDY GUIDE, READ
pages 43–52 of *The Journey.*

> *More than anything in life, we need to find the right path for*
> *our journey through life—but is it possible? Does it even exist?*
> *The right path is His path, and that is the path we need to seek.*
> BILLY GRAHAM
> *The Journey*

THINK ABOUT IT

The Son of God became a man to enable men to become
sons of God.

—C. S. LEWIS[1]

You have made known to me the path of life;
you will fill me
with joy in your presence,
with eternal pleasures at your right hand.

—PSALM 16:11

Life is full of "I wish I would have" moments. So many times we wish for second chances following the unfavorable results of a thought or action. Many people make the mistake of believing they never can change directions. Both lines of thought lead to the same result—hopelessness. Have you been there? Are you there right now?

Have you given up hope that life can be any different? Have you tried everything you know and still see no change? Maybe you're looking at the wrong path. There is a right path, but it might not be one of the paths you are considering.

REWIND

Which of the following have you tried, thinking that they might solve one or more of the problems you face? (Check all that apply.)

_____ Education

_____ Money

_____ Success

_____ Social standing

_____ Entertainment

_____ Psychology

_____ Spirituality

_____ Self-help books

_____ Relationships

_____ Employment

_____ Other: _____

Some of these things have a place in our lives, but apart from a relationship with God, they are powerless to do anything more than frustrate us. Alone they cannot take us to the right path for our lives. There is a right path—a path provided by God. But how can we find it? It begins by discovering your greatest need.

What is your greatest need?

_____

What are some things you do in an effort to meet that need?

_____

_____

_____

In order to get on the right path, you must acknowledge the fact that you are on the wrong path. The wrong path is the result of sin—the universal problem. Everyone must choose to change paths or, by default, they choose to remain alienated from God. You can't get to God on your present path. That's a truth our culture seems to resist. Many people desire to have a relationship with God, but they believe they can get to Him without changing anything in their lives.

Read Matthew 7:13. What does Jesus say in response to the belief that people can get to God without changing paths?

_____

_____

_____

Read Jeremiah 6:16. What does this Scripture passage say about the issue?

_____

_____

_____

The end result of never changing paths is insecurity, chaos, and destruction—eternal destruction. Therefore our greatest need isn't material; it is spiritual. Our greatest need isn't trading one socioeconomic status for another; it is trading our sinful nature for a new nature. That is the path God designed for each of us.

> *What happened in Eden was a preview of what happens to us every day. Adam and Eve's decision is repeated by every generation and by every person. We all are guilty of sin, because we all choose our own way instead of God's way. Never lose sight of the seriousness of sin. Its corruption has affected everything: our bodies, our minds, our emotions, our wills, our souls, our institutions, our world—everything.*
>
> BILLY GRAHAM
> *The Journey*

JOURNEY THROUGH GOD'S WORD

We talk a lot about sin, but sometimes we have a difficult time understanding the concept behind the word. Technically, sin is rebelling against God. It is the end result of surrendering to anything other than God's control of our lives.

The Bible presents several different views of sin. One Old Testament concept is the act of breaking the law of God. Deuteronomy 6:24–25 defines a righteous person as one who keeps God's law. It stands to reason, therefore, that an unrighteous person would be one who failed to keep God's law. Someone who is unrighteous would be considered sinful.[2]

Sin also is viewed in the Old Testament as anything done that is outside the boundaries of God's nature. Leviticus 11:45 calls for God's people to imitate His holiness. Failing to do so means falling short of God's standards for our lives. By definition, falling short of God's standards is sin.[3]

God's relationship with His people was established and governed by covenants. In their spiritually strong times, the Israelites ceremonially renewed their commitment to keeping the covenant with God. Anything that was outside of the boundaries of the covenant would fall into the category of sin (see Deuteronomy 29:19–21).

The New Testament concept of sin was much the same as the Old Testament with a couple of additions. In the New Testament, sin is anything that disrupts one's fellowship with God. Jesus pointed out that the mind (or heart) is where sin originates. Visible actions are not sin, but the visible effects of sin. There are a variety of Greek words used to describe specific actions or attitudes that all are sin. Some examples are *trespass, lawlessness, evil, uncleanness, unrighteousness, unbelief,* and *lust*.

The bottom line is that sin is anything that separates man from God. The only remedy for the condition is a change of heart—salvation! Even then, the consequences of sin are long-lasting. Every sin is first a sin against God. However, there also are personal and social consequences. People become enslaved to sin; societies become depraved. Our present personal and social conditions are direct results of sin in our lives and our world.[4]

Have you changed paths? Are you walking confidently on the path God provides? Do you understand that there is only one source for real hope? What difference is it making in your daily life?

_____

_____

_____

_____

_____

_____

Read James 2:10. What does it say about the idea that we can live sinless lives?

_____

_____

_____

_____

What hope do we have? Our only hope for eternal salvation is found in Jesus Christ. This was God's plan all along. He saw you and your condition long before you were born. His love for you moved Him to provide a way for you to have a permanent relationship with Him. But God's plan wasn't just for the afterlife; it is for your daily life.

Read John 14:6. What is God's only plan?

_____

_____

_____

_____

How can this plan produce peace in today's world?

_____

_____

_____

_____

_____

All you need to do is choose a path. Choose to stay on the old path and live with the consequences of that choice. Choose to walk the new path—God's path—and enjoy the present and future benefits of that choice.

RETHINK

No other person in history has made a lasting impact like that made by Jesus Christ. Ancient history and the Bible confirm Jesus' existence. Jesus is the foundation and the focus of the Christian faith. We make a mistake if we base our knowledge of our faith on the words of preachers, writers, speakers, or denominations! Our knowledge of our faith must be based on God's revelation in His Word and through His Son.

Who was Jesus?

_____ A prophet

_____ A simple man

_____ A spiritual phenomenon

_____ Fully God and fully man

_____ None of the above

Reread John 14:6. How does this verse compare to your response to the previous question?

_____

_____

_____

_____

The Bible tells us that Jesus was God in human form. Why is this a difficult concept to grasp? It's tough to see God as a human. It's also tough to see a human as God. Yet, both are true! Just because we can't comprehend it doesn't make it untrue.

> *The Bible (the source of our information about Jesus) tells us something that staggers our imagination. It tells us that Jesus was God in human form. He was a man, fully and completely. But He was more than that: He was also God. He was not just a godly man; He was God Himself, wrapped in human flesh. Never forget: That baby born in Bethlehem's stable was not a son of God (only one among many)—He was the Son of God, uniquely sent from the Father to become our Savior from sin.*
>
> BILLY GRAHAM
> *The Journey*

Read John 1:1, 14. According to these verses, who was Jesus?

_____

_____

_____

Jesus was more than a godly man; He was more than a manly God. He was everything that God is and everything that we are. We know what others have said about Jesus, but what does the Bible say about Him?

Read the following Scriptures and summarize what each verse
says about Jesus. By whom was each statement made?

John 10:30

_____

_____

_____

John 14:9

_____

_____

_____

Matthew 17:5

_____

_____

_____

Knowing who Jesus was is important, but we also must understand what He did.

REFLECT

Why would God's Son leave heaven to come live on the earth only to be mistreated, doubted, and eventually killed? He did it for one reason: to save us from our sin. He came to do what we cannot do for ourselves. Jesus came to make the ultimate trade . . . in exchange for our sins He offers His Spirit. Jesus was treated just like common criminals of His day; He was crucified on a Roman cross. There are four ways to look at the events surrounding the crucifixion of Jesus Christ.

1. **Jesus was the sacrifice for sin.**

   The sacrifice for sin is a common element in world religions of all kinds. History teaches us that religion always has sought to provide a way for people to deal with their sins. In the Old Testament, God accepted the appropriate animal sacrifice as an offering for sin. However, the sacrifices were situational—that is, they covered a specific sin. Any future sins required additional sacrifices.

   The sacrificial system became cumbersome and was complicated by a legal structure that made it almost impossible for someone to be in a right relationship with God. But Jesus' sacrifice did something the animal sacrifice could never do.

Read Hebrews 9:26. What was different about Jesus' sacrifice?

_____

_____

_____

2. **Jesus was our substitute.**

    God cannot look on sin. Therefore, He cannot even look at a person who has sinned. That leaves little hope for all of us. In order to keep each of us from having to pay for our sins, Jesus paid with His life. He was our substitute.

Read Genesis 22:1–19. How difficult would it be for you to offer a sacrifice similar to the one Abraham offered?

Very easy |----------|----------|----------|----------| Impossible

Offering His Son wasn't easy for God. Yet He did it because He loves you and doesn't want you to miss out on an eternity with Him in heaven.

Read 2 Corinthians 5:21. How does it make you feel to know that God paid the debt you could not pay?

_____

_____

_____

If it weren't for God's grace, how could you avoid His judgment? You couldn't! You'd have no hope.

3. **Jesus was our Redeemer.**

    In the ancient world, captured soldiers could be freed only by the payment of a ransom. Every person is born into sin's captivity. Only the payment of a ransom can set you free.

Read Matthew 20:28 and 1 Timothy 2:5–6. Who paid your ransom?

_____ You

_____ Your parents

_____ Jesus Christ

_____ Your ransom is unpaid.

The ransom wasn't paid to Satan; it was divine payment required to satisfy God. Without the payment of the ransom, you and I would be required to stand before God in judgment. Jesus paid the debt for each of us.

4. **Jesus was our Conqueror.**

When Jesus was on the cross, many people thought Satan had won the battle between good and evil. Even those who were the closest to Jesus thought He was dead. What once had been hope quickly disintegrated into hopelessness. But the resurrection changed everything. Hope was renewed, and victory over death was realized.

Read Colossians 2:15. Over whom or what was Jesus victorious?

_____

_____

_____

_____

> *By His death and resurrection, Jesus became our sacrifice . . .*
> *our substitute . . . our redeemer . . . our conqueror. He did*
> *for us what we could never do for ourselves—and He did it*
> *out of love. Think of it: He loves you so much that He was will-*
> *ing to give His life for you! Now He offers you salvation as a*
> *free gift—free because He has already paid for it. He wants to*
> *forgive your past and set your feet on a new path—His path.*
> BILLY GRAHAM
> *The Journey*

For those who believe in Jesus Christ, the issue is settled. There is no reason to fear eternity. There is no reason to live without hope. Jesus conquered sin once and for all, and we are fellow conquerors if we accept Him as our Savior and Lord.

REACT

What will you do with Jesus? It's your choice. Jesus will never force Himself on anyone. His offer of forgiveness and eternal life is yours for the taking.

What must you do?

	Done	Needed
1. Repent of your sins.	____	____
2. Believe in Jesus Christ.	____	____
3. Commit yourself to follow Christ.	____	____

Though these are "once in a lifetime" decisions, they all require constant attention. Daily we must confess our sins to Christ, trust in His leadership, and follow Him willingly. If you haven't taken the steps above, now is your opportunity.

1. **Repent of your sins.**

   Repent means "to change directions." With God's help you can change what's controlling you. You can make the shift from being controlled by sin to being controlled by God. It is more than feeling sorry about your sin; it is choosing to admit your need for forgiveness.

2. **Believe in Jesus Christ and what He did for you.**

   Believing is more than acknowledging fact. It includes an element of trust. Trust means placing your confidence in something. You don't inherit trust; you choose to trust. John 1:12 tells us that receiving Christ is a requirement for salvation.

3. Commit yourself to follow Christ.

Becoming a Christian happens in a moment; *being* a Christian is a lifelong journey.

Are you ready to make that commitment to Christ? Are you ready to accept His offer of forgiveness and eternal life? If so, you can pray a prayer similar to the one that follows. There are no magic words here, just an example of what your prayer might be.

O God, I know I am a sinner. I am sorry for my sins, and I want to turn from them. I trust Christ alone as my Savior, and I confess Him as my Lord. From this moment on, I want to serve Him and follow Him in the fellowship of His church. In Christ's name I pray, amen.

If you prayed that prayer and meant it, you are now a child of God. Everything we've learned in this lesson is now true about you!

Accepting Christ isn't the end but the beginning—the beginning of a whole new life on God's path. Don't let anything keep you from that commitment.

BILLY GRAHAM
The Journey

What are three truths you learned in this study, and how will you apply each truth to your daily life?

1. _____

_____

_____

_____

2. _____

_____

_____

_____

3. _____

_____

_____

_____

6

A New
Beginning

T O GET THE MOST FROM THIS STUDY GUIDE, READ
pages 53–62 of *The Journey.*

*When we come to Christ, God gives us a whole new life: a new
relationship, a new citizenship, a new family, a new purpose, a
new power, a new destiny.*

BILLY GRAHAM
The Journey

THINK ABOUT IT

*Sanctification is the work of Christ in me, the sign that I am
no longer independent, but completely dependent on Him.*

—OSWALD CHAMBERS[1]

*He who was seated on the throne said, "I am making every-
thing new!"*

—REVELATION 21:5

Starting over is something we all wish we could do at times. If you've ever been working on a project and made a mistake, you might have been forced to start over. But can we start over in life? Can we erase the past and start with a fresh slate today? Some people might argue that we can't, but the Bible teaches that we can.

What are the advantages of starting over? They are immeasurable! What are the advantages of staying on the path you're on—if you don't know Christ? They are nonexistent! In Revelation 21:5, Jesus declared that He has the power to make all things new. A day is coming when all things will be made new. But you don't have to wait for that day; newness can be yours today.

What if you already have accepted Jesus Christ as your Lord and Savior? This lesson still has an application in your life. Salvation is a once-in-a-lifetime event, but sanctification is an ongoing process. Salvation might be in the past, but sanctification is your present and future.

REWIND

Which of the following statements best describes you?

_____ I was raised in a Christian home and met Jesus Christ when I was a child.

_____ I was raised in a Christian home and met Jesus Christ when I was a teen.

_____ I was raised in a Christian home but have not accepted Jesus Christ as Lord.

_____ I wasn't raised in a Christian home but met Jesus Christ when I was a child.

_____ I wasn't raised in a Christian home but met Jesus Christ when I was teen.

_____ I wasn't raised in a Christian home and have not accepted Jesus Christ as Lord.

_____ I accepted Jesus Christ as Lord when I was an adult.

_____ I don't think a person must accept Jesus Christ in order to go to heaven.

_____ I don't know whether or not I have accepted Jesus Christ as Lord of my life.

_____ Other: _____

There is a common thread among the choices above—they all have something to do with accepting Jesus Christ as Savior and Lord. The decision to accept His offer of salvation is the most important decision in a person's life.

What have been three of your most important decisions in life?

_____

_____

_____

Before now, would the decision to accept Jesus Christ as Savior have made the list? Why or why not?

_____

_____

_____

Every journey has a starting point. This is true of your journey with Christ. A man named Saul met Jesus Christ in dramatic fashion (see Acts 22:7). The transformation in Saul's life even included a change of name—to Paul. Paul would become the missionary who started many of the churches mentioned in the New Testament and the author of many of the books in the New Testament. What Paul was before his conversion isn't important; the important thing is what he became.

Forget about your past. What is God accomplishing in and through your life right now?

_____

_____

_____

It's not important how you came to Christ. Nor does it matter what you did before you came to Christ. The only thing that matters is that you have accepted Him as your Lord and Savior. If you haven't done that, you have no promise of eternal life in heaven. You have no possibility for peace on this earth. And you have no relationship with the Creator of this world and all that is in it.

> *People come to Christ in many different ways; your experience won't necessarily be like mine. Some conversions are sudden and dramatic, a radical change from one way of living to another. Others come to Christ more slowly, perhaps not even knowing exactly when they have crossed the line from unbelief to belief. The important thing is not how we come to Christ, but that we do come, and that we are sure we are now trusting Christ for our salvation. Are you certain of your commitment to Him?*
>
> BILLY GRAHAM
> *The Journey*

Read 2 Corinthians 6:2. When should you come to Christ?

_____ When I'm old

_____ When I've run out of other options

_____ Now

_____ Never

Have you done this? If not, why not?

_____

_____

_____

JOURNEY THROUGH GOD'S WORD

Salvation is one of those terms we use a lot but is often misunderstood. In the Bible, salvation includes three ideas. The first is being rescued from danger. Danger might be in the form of physical danger. It also can mean rescue from the danger posed by death and sin. The second idea involves spiritual renewal. This is God's response to humanity's fallen state. Moral integrity is impossible apart from

---

God's Spirit. The third concept is the reconciliation between God and man. When sin entered the world, the relationship between man and God was fractured. Though man might try, the restoration of that relationship must be initiated by God. Salvation is God's way to mend the broken relationship. God's desire for reconciliation is summed up in Romans 5:10. Rescue, renewal, and reconciliation are all a part of the work of God through Jesus Christ.[2]

In the Old Testament, salvation often is physical with spiritual applications, while in the New Testament it is spiritual with physical applications. The early part of the Old Testament story shows God's efforts to save the nation of Israel. In the Psalms, the focus of salvation shifts from national to personal.

The foundational principles behind salvation are consistent—God's holiness and intolerance for sin, and God's unchanging love and mercy. People, on the other hand, are viewed as sinful and unable to save themselves. Both testaments show humanity's need and God's provision. Salvation isn't needed if you aren't in danger. The very fact that God offers salvation means that we all are in danger—in danger of spending eternity separated from God in a real place called hell. We also are in danger of languishing in a life that is meaningless and empty. Salvation offers encouragement for the present and hope for the future.

Has it been a while since you first met Christ? Is your relationship with Jesus more or less dynamic than it was when you first met Him? Explain the change.

_____

_____

_____

Read 2 Corinthians 5:17. What does this verse say to you?

_____

_____

_____

God said that you are a new creation—redesigned from the inside out. The spiritual transformation affects every area of life. Maybe you know someone who has experienced this radical transformation. You might know someone whose change was less dramatic; maybe you have had an experience like this yourself. The fact remains that anyone who knows Jesus Christ as Lord and Savior will never be the same.

So, what happens? How does this spiritual transformation impact your daily life? Let's look at some of the results.

RETHINK

We know that God makes all things new. But let's take a look at seven specific things that happen (and continue to happen) in the lives of those who give their lives to Jesus Christ.

1. **A New Relationship**
   Take a look at the following verses of Scripture. Summarize each one in your own words:

   <u>BEFORE (Ephesians 2:12)</u>

   _____

   _____

   _____

   <u>AFTER (Romans 5:1)</u>

   _____

   _____

   _____

In this new relationship, you have moved from being God's enemy to being His friend. In addition, you now have the privilege of being called a child of God.

What are the benefits associated with being a child of God?

_____

_____

_____

What are the responsibilities associated with being a child of God?

_____

_____

_____

Match the following verses with their statements: [Answers can be found at the end of the chapter.]

a. You are born again through God's Word.

b. You are adopted into God's family.

c. You must be born again.

d. You must imitate God.

_____ Ephesians 5:1   _____ John 3:4

_____ Ephesians 1:5   _____ 1 Peter 1:23

These are strong instructions, not suggestions. They are true; you must choose to obey or disobey them.

2. **A New Citizenship**

   As a believer, you are a citizen of the kingdom of God. There are certain privileges that accompany your new citizenship.

What are some of the privileges and responsibilities of citizenship in your nation?

_____

_____

_____

What are some of the privileges and responsibilities of citizenship in the kingdom of God?

_____

_____

_____

Read Philippians 3:20 and Acts 5:29. What should you do if you find yourself in a situation where man's laws and God's laws are in opposition?

_____

_____

_____

One day, the earth as we know it will pass away and the kingdom of God will remain. Those who are citizens of the kingdom of God will live in peace with God and each other. Those who are not citizens of the kingdom of God will spend eternity separated from God in hell. Therefore the citizenship decision you make today has eternal consequences.

3. A New Family

Many people trace their family lineage several generations. They tediously pour over historical records in an attempt to discover their family trees. Some discover they are related to significant historical figures. Others trace generations only to discover that their family tree has no superstars. Well, becoming a Christian won't change your genetic relationships, but it does make you a member of a larger universal family—the family of God!

You aren't just related to God; you are now related to other believers. We are bound together in God's family, not by an organization but by a spiritual relationship. When you think of church, you probably think of a particular building or group of people, or perhaps your own denomination. But the church is far greater than this. It includes the whole family of God—that vast unseen fellowship of men and women throughout the ages who belong to Christ. This is one reason why you are never alone if you know Christ.

BILLY GRAHAM
The Journey

In 1 Timothy 3:15, Paul referred to God's household as the church. How would you describe your commitment to your church? (Place an X on the line.)

Poor |------------|------------|-------------|------------| Excellent

What can you do to improve your commitment to your church?

_____

_____

_____

Notice, the responsibility for improving your commitment to the church rests on you. Many people expect the church to conform to their needs, yet that isn't the picture painted in the New Testament. The church is the collective body of Christ assembled together to worship Him.

4. A New Purpose

What is your purpose in life? There has been a lot written on this topic, so the question is something many people have considered. But even many Christians separate their purposes in life from their spiritual lives. When you accept Jesus Christ as Lord, you receive a new purpose in life—His purpose.

Why does God leave people on earth after they are saved?

_____ To do what they want to do

_____ To do what He wants them to do

_____ To aggravate the rest of us!

God had a plan for you before you were born. It is the best plan—the plan that will lead to a life you never imagined. It might not be the life you envisioned, but there is no life more rewarding than the life God intended for you. Paul told the Ephesians that they were "created . . . to do good works, which God prepared in advance for us to do" (Ephesians 2:10).

What "good works" has God prepared for you to do?

_____

_____

_____

Are you doing these works? If not, why not?

_____

_____

_____

5. A New Power

When you become a Christian, God moves in and brings with Him His power. God's presence in the life of a believer is His Holy Spirit. It was the Holy Spirit who first made you aware of your need for God in your life. When God gives you a new purpose, He also gives you the power to achieve your purpose by His Holy Spirit.

Stop and think for a moment about the fact that God empowers you for His purposes. How does that make you feel?

_____

_____

_____

Read Romans 8:9. What is the proof that you belong to Christ?

_____ Owning a large Bible

_____ Having perfect church attendance

_____ Having a leadership role in your church

_____ Having the Spirit of Christ in your life

It is easy to equate emotion with the Spirit of Christ. Some people believe that God is not at work in their lives unless they are emotional. According to the Bible, God's Spirit comes to live in us the moment we come to Christ. When God comes to live in us, we have access to His power in our lives (see Acts 1:8). In addition, the Bible also teaches that the Spirit of God never leaves us!

REFLECT

The five gifts mentioned already are present-centered. That is, they should be evident in the everyday lives of believers. The sixth gift is more future-centered.

6. A New Destiny

When you come to know Christ, your eternal destination is dramatically changed. Scripture teaches that there are only two places in which your soul can spend eternity—heaven or hell. Before you accept Jesus Christ as Savior, your destination is hell. Once you accept Him, your destination immediately and permanently changes! You are destined for eternity in heaven with God!

Eternal life is a gift. Take a look at Romans 6:23. There is nothing you can do to earn eternal life. You can't be good enough or trust that you are better than someone else.

Read 1 Peter 1:3–4. How durable is your salvation?

_____ It disappears the moment I have a bad thought or say something I shouldn't.

_____ It stays as long as I am better than other people.

_____ It will never perish, spoil, or fade—it is permanent.

Regardless of the trials you face in this life, your eternal destiny is secure and certain—heaven! How does that make you feel?

_____

_____

_____

_____

REACT

So, what now? We still have one more gift to discuss . . . the gift of a new journey.

7. **A New Journey**

Your faith in Christ provides everything we've discussed so far, which can be summed up in the concept of a new journey. With so many people living to please themselves, the Christian journey has a different focus. It is a focus on serving and pleasing God. It is a lifelong journey of discipleship and maturity.

What is the difference between *becoming* a Christian and *being* a Christian?

_____

_____

_____

_____

_____

You now get to decide if you will allow your life to be lived out in obedience to God's plan for your life or if you will try things your way. The benefits of living for Christ are explained in this lesson. The consequences of trying to live on your own also are obvious—the opposite of everything discussed in this lesson. The choice is yours; what is your decision?

> *The Christian life is a new journey—one that will take us the rest of our lives. And the best part is this: We never walk it alone for Christ walks with us.*
>
> BILLY GRAHAM
> *The Journey*

What are three truths you learned in this study, and how will you apply each truth to your daily life?

1. _____

_____

_____

_____

2. _____

_____

_____

_____

3. _____

_____

_____

_____

Answers to Scripture matching on page 116 —

a. 1 Peter 1:23; b. Ephesians 1:5; c. John 3:4; d. Ephesians 5:1

NOTES

CHAPTER 1

1. Bob Kelly, *Worth Repeating*, 2003. Grand Rapids, MI: Kregel Publications, 139.

2. Rosamund Stone Zander and Benjamin Zander, *The Art of Possibility*, 2002. New York: Penguin Books, 18.

CHAPTER 2

1. Bob Kelly, *Worth Repeating*, 140.

CHAPTER 3

1. Bob Kelly, *Worth Repeating*, 141.

CHAPTER 4

1. Bob Kelly, *Worth Repeating*, 221.

2. *Holman Illustrated Bible Dictionary*, 2003. Nashville, TN: B&H, 999.

CHAPTER 5

1. Bob Kelly, *Worth Repeating*, 304.

2. *Holman Illustrated Bible Dictionary*, 1505.

3. Ibid.

4. Ibid., 1506–1507.

CHAPTER 6

1. Bob Kelly, *Worth Repeating*, 305.

2. *Holman Illustrated Bible Dictionary*, 1435.

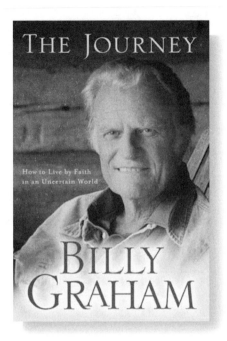

Billy Graham is respected and loved around the world.
The Journey is his magnum opus, the culmination of a
lifetime of experience and ministry. With insight that comes
only from a life spent with God, this book is filled with
wisdom, encouragement, hope, and inspiration for anyone
who wants to live a happier, more fulfilling life.

978-0-8499-1887-2 (PB)

STUDY GUIDE NOTES

STUDY GUIDE NOTES

STUDY GUIDE NOTES

STUDY GUIDE NOTES

_____

_____

_____

_____

_____

_____

_____

_____

_____

_____

_____

_____

_____

_____

_____

_____

_____

_____

_____

_____

_____

_____

_____

STUDY GUIDE NOTES